OVERCOMERS INSTITUTE

"THE GOVERNMENT OF THE KINGDOM"

"DELIVERANCE 099 – LOCK-UP"

"INCIPIENT – PROPHETIC COURSE LEVEL 1"

GOVERNMENTAL GIFTS

APOSTLE CHRISTIAN T. HOWELL SR.

The Government of the Kingdom

CHRISTIAN T. HOWELL SR.

vercomers

GOVERNMENTAL GIFTS

CHURCH GOVERNMENT
FIVE FOLD MINISTRY

TEACHERS

PROPHETS

APOSTLES

1 Corinthians 12:28

PASTORS

EVANGELISTS

CHURCH GOVERNMENT
ESTABLISHED BY OUR LORD JESUS CHRIST

_____

_____

_____

_____

_____

_____

Government =

1: a politically organized community or major territorial unit having a monarchical form of government headed by a king or queen

2: the eternal kingship of God

3: a realm or region in which something is dominant

4: an area or sphere in which one holds a preeminent position

A government is the system or group of people governing an organized community, often a state.

Every government has a kind of constitution, a statement of its governing principles and philosophy.

Monarchy vs Democracy

Monarchy – an autocracy governed by a monarch who usually inherits the authority – ruled by one person

Democracy – majority rule: the doctrine that the numerical majority of an organized group can make decisions binding on the whole group – ruled by the majority

_____

_____

_____

_____

_____

Theocracy – a form of government in which a god or deity is recognized as the state's supreme civil ruler, or in a broader sense, a form of government in which a state is governed by immediate divine guidance or by officials who are regarded as divinely guided.

Kingdom = basileia (Greek)
Phonetic Spelling: (bas-il-i'-ah)
Short Definition: kingship, sovereignty, authority, rule, kingdom

　　　properly, kingdom; the realm in which a king sovereignly rules.

A KINGDOM ALWAYS REQUIRES A KING

Church = ekklésia
Phonetic Spelling: (ek-klay-see'-ah)
Short Definition: an assembly, congregation, church

ek, "out from and to" and kaléō, "to call") – properly, people called out from the world and to God, the outcome being the Church (the mystical body of Christ) – i.e. the universal (total) body of believers whom God calls out from the world and into His eternal kingdom.

[The English word "church" comes from the Greek word kyriakos, "belonging to the Lord" (kyrios). Ekklēsía ("church") is the root of the terms "ecclesiology" and "ecclesiastical."]

Church =
an assembly of the people convened at the public place of council for the purpose of deliberating or making policy and decisions. They came together to elect officials, to declare war, and to form policy for the operation of the city.

Matthew 6:10

(**KJV**) Thy kingdom come, Thy will be done in earth, as it is in heaven.

(**TPT**) Manifest your kingdom realm, and cause your every purpose to be fulfilled on earth, just as it is fulfilled in heaven.

(**MSG**) Set the world right; Do what's best— as above, so below.

_____

_____

_____

_____

On Earth, Jesus was the full expression of the government of heaven. When he ascended, he left "gifts" that would become the full expression of Kingdom Government on Earth. I'd like to call them the "governors".

_____

_____

_____

TEACHER
"THE GROUNDER"

Teacher = didaskalos = instructor, teacher, doctor

Teacher = nomosdidaskalos = an expounder or teacher or rabbi who minister of the law of god

Teaches principles, prescriptions, and regulations

Establishes principles & standards; develops learning & teaching formulas, and drafts rules of application and usage with methodology

Effectively imparts knowledge to others – results in getting knowledge

_____

_____

_____

FUNCTIONS

Course development

Lesson planning & preparation

Developing people

Learning assessments

_____

_____

_____

PERSONALITY

Diligence, intuition, insight, & empathy

Order, methodology, & procedural

Strong organization, structure, leadership & interactive

Good planning & implementation

Excellent communication & listening skills

Strong command of audience of audience/students

Knack for inspiring learning & growth

Commitment, conscientiousness, & faithfulness

Hungry for knowledge & eager to learn

Capacity for taking in huge amounts of information, sifting & sorting thru it

Understand why people avoid learning & what makes it difficult for some to learn

Structured, orderly thinkers who deliberate extensively over new facts

Inclined towards research & investigation of facts

Methodical

Tenderness towards learning deficiencies and the problems that cause or intensify them

A commitment to student progress & learning success

Critical thinker w/ a deep desire to solve the problems they encounter

Recognize the need for basic controls, authority, and organization to a mission; usually respects procedures outlined by administration

Rely on creativity and innovation

TEACHER

Strengths: Education addresses one's citizenship, work, society, & culture

Enhances prosperity & productivity

Pitfalls: lack of preparation; overly didactic; humanistic doctrine & methodologies

_____

_____

_____

_____

_____

_____

_____

_____

_____

EVANGELIST

"THE BIRTHER OR THE GATHERER"

Evangelist = eu (good or well) or ev (life or live

Evangelist = chayah = eve, giver of life

Evangelist= good messenger of well-being & life or a life filled with well-being

"Life-givers"… cause people to live by reviving them

Implants what is needed to keep people from death and leave them with the gift of eternal life

Brings recovery, reparation, & restoration…bringing them into covenant with God

_____

_____

_____

FUNCTIONS

Wrestles & struggles in prayer with hosts of darkness and unbelief to herd the lost

Preaches conversion; steers them into the church

1st line introduction to the lord

Underground warrior snatching souls

_____

_____

_____

PERSONALITY

Energetic, fervent, & driven by the burden for the lost

Bold, courageous, & dedicated...forceful – risk-taker

Sensitive & fiery personality; highly emotional & passionate

Dutiful & studious

Outgoing, personable, & people-oriented

Compassionate & merciful

Dynamic, itinerant

Miraculous & highly charged

Confrontational & warring

Outreach oriented & global minded

Militant & combatant

Strong inter-community activities

Extensive intercession & travail

Emphasis on preaching

Pitfall: usually resort to preaching the salvation...the cross. This is only problematic because more mature converts need a different diet

---

PASTOR

"THE SHEPHERD OR "THE GUARD"

Pastor = roei (hebrew) = shepherd

Pastor = poimen (greek) = shepherd

Shepherds are marked by ruling, government, supervision, & intimate association with the flock

Finds and maintains suitable pasture for the sheep

Watchful over their moral & spiritual conduct

Concerned with nururing, growth, protection, & safety

Companion, consoler, & comforter of the flock

_____

_____

_____

FUNCTIONS

Assures safety of the flock; elements & environments

Uses:

Cloak – a covering & a resource. It provides warmtn – but also becomes secutiry to a new sheep

Rod – emblem of power & weapon of defense. It is synonymous with a scepter

Staff – instrument of support & discipline. It holds the shepherd steady as he climbs & navigates, the hook pulls the sheep back in

Close and constant presence is the essence of management of the sheep

Success of shepherd relies on obedience of sheep

Shepherds live with/among the sheep

Knows the sheep, as a group & as individuals

Values the pairing of sheep… helps accountability

Great intimacy with the sheep… they know each other beyond surface level

_____

_____

_____

_____

_____

PERSONALITY & TRAITS

May or may not be the founder of church

Can pastor several churches at a time

Emphasizes post conversion care of sheep (can handle adopted or inherited sheep)

Deeply involved in the life of the sheep…even if it's not their personal desire to do

Aims to mature, stabilize, & enrich the sheep's life

Order, authority, government, organization, and leadership are mandatory characteristics

Sometimes firm, even stern. But their over-involvement & intimate knowledge sometimes cause bias & preferential treatment among sheep…usually shields who is weaker

Nurturing, development, liberty, holiness, and discipleship are their priorities

Teaching anointing is needed for this office/gift

People-oriented and congregation minded. They live with their people more than any other office! They are paternal or maternal in nature

Committed to biblical knowledge & spiritual insight (based on feeding requirements)

Critical thinking, situation analysis, evaluation, & problem solving skills are required

Protectors & guardian of the flock

Impeccable morality, ethics, & integrity

Great fortitude, rectitude, perseverance, & character

Loyal, humble, & meek

Christian maturity & stability

_____

_____

_____

_____

_____

_____

APOSTLE

"THE SENT ONE OR THE GOVERNOR"

Apostle = shaliach (HEBREW) = sent messenger

Apostle = apostolos (GREEK) = Envoy, ambassador, or messenger commissioned to carry out the instructions of the commissioning agent

Verb apostello, referring to the sending of a fleet or an embassy

sets in motion, not responds to, what takes place on earth

_____

_____

_____

FUNCTIONS

Adminstering doctrine & solidifying fellowship

Provoking fear on opposers and guarding the church

Working supernatural signs and wonders to turn people from satan to god

Judging & governing sin in the church

Teaching the word of god

Exposing heresy; guarding truth

Preparing & empowering other ministers

Manifesting the truth of god generation to generation

Goes and takes back what was stolen for god

An ambassador who is dispatched to a foreign field to handle the affairs, settle the accounts, and negotiate agreements in the best interests of the one who sent him

Operates outside of the routine to execute and officiate a new thing

ADVANCING THE KINGDOM OF GOD=

ACTS 26:18

1. To open the eyes (of mankind)

2. To turn them from darkness to light

3. To turn them from the power of satan to god…

> That they may receive forgiveness of sin

> That they may receive an inheritance with the sanctified ones

Apostles are sent to aggressively take back what was stolen. To support their mandate, they are given enormous powers and supernatural support.

Apostles are forewarned & forearmed.

Apostles are never docile, rarely quiet, and never easy on the nerves or soothing to the norm or status quo.

PERSONALITY & TRAITS

High capacity for envisioning & effective planning

Strong teaching/preaching ministry

Capacity for long-range planning

Strong developmental & disciplinarian bent; superior at confrontations

Commendable teaching, evaluative skills, and piercing discernment

Straightforward about problem resolution and are quick to change techniques

Possess superior prophetic abilities balanced by practical wisdom and grasp of the mind of the lord

Keen understanding of leadership, organization and government

Mission & outreach minded, with global emphasis

Motivated by god's pleasure; usually bruised internally…preparing them for the nature of separation and extraction

Possess a deep affection for the lord

Power – latent, dormant, overt, and dynamic – characterize the office

Authority is the main feature of credibility; captures attention & commands respect

Judicial (not judgmental), executive, and administrative in nature

Multi-strata, not dual... secular training often gives roots & advantages

_____

_____

_____

_____

_____

_____

_____

_____

_____

_____

SPIRITUAL GIFTS

Motivational Gifts that stimulate the unique drives within the believer

Manifestation Gifts of the Holy Spirit's anointing, channeled through the believer's life, on precise occasion as He chooses

Ministry Gifts, or the position the believer has in the work of the Body of Christ, the Church) – are all for every believer to experience.

THREE REVEALTION GIFTS:

1. *"A Word of Wisdom"* God-given supernatural "knowing" what to do, or say, in some particular situation.

2. *"A Word of Knowledge"* God-given supernatural "facts" from the mind of God.

3. *"Discerning of spirits"* God-given "discernment" into the spirit world.

THREE POWER GIFTS:

1. *"Faith"* God-given "ability to expect" an extraordinary demonstration of the power of God

2. *"Miracles"* God-given "intervention" in the ordinary course of nature to work His will.

3. *"Gifts of Healing"* God-given belief in praying for the sickness, diseases and infirmities.

_____

_____

_____

THREE SPOKEN GIFTS

1. *"Tongues"* God-given supernatural utterance in an unknown language.

2. *"Interpretation"* God-given supernatural showing forth the meaning of the unknown tongue.

3. *"Prophecy"* God-given inspiration to give His message, supernaturally.

_____

_____

_____

DELIVERANCE 099
"LOCK-UP"
CHRISTIAN T. HOWELL SR.

Matthew 12:28 (KJV) But if I cast out devils by the Spirit of God, then the kingdom of God is come unto you.

Matthew 12:28 (MSG) "But if it's by God's power that I am sending the evil spirits packing, then God's kingdom is here for sure.

 - Deliverance is a mandate and function of the Kingdom. It is an expression and authority function of Kingdom authority.

_____

_____

_____

_____

_____

_____

Matthew 15:21-28 (KJV)

21 Then Jesus went thence, and departed into the coasts of Tyre and Sidon.

22 And, behold, a woman of Canaan came out of the same coasts, and cried unto him, saying, Have mercy on me, O Lord, thou Son of David; my **daughter is grievously vexed with a devil.**

23 But he answered her not a word. And his disciples came and besought him, saying, Send her away; for she crieth after us.

24 But he answered and said, I am not sent but unto the lost sheep of the house of Israel.

25 Then came she and worshipped him, saying, Lord, help me.

26 But he answered and said, It is not meet to take the **children's bread**, and to cast it to dogs.

27 And she said, Truth, Lord: yet the dogs **eat of the crumbs** which fall from their masters' table.

28 Then Jesus answered and said unto her, O woman, great is thy faith: be it unto thee even as thou wilt. **And her daughter was made whole from that very hour.**

- Bread is, and was, a main part of their daily diet. It was eaten at almost every meal dating back to the passover and exodus from Egypt.

- "The children's bread" indicates that deliverance is not just for sinners or people who are "not saved".

- "The children" can and do need deliverance!

- Deliverance should be administered and received as often as necessary.

- It is the right of every follower of Jesus Christ to partake in deliverance.

- Deliverance enables wholeness.

_____

_____

Mark 16:15-18 (KJV)

15 And he said unto them, Go ye into all the world, and preach the gospel to every creature.

16 He that believeth and is baptized shall be saved; but he that believeth not shall be damned.

17 And these signs shall follow them that believe; In my name shall they cast out devils; they shall speak with new tongues;

18 They shall take up serpents; and if they drink any deadly thing, it shall not hurt them; they shall lay hands on the sick, and they shall recover.

- "The Great Commission" was given to all believers
- Deliverance ministry is not reserved for the few "religious and spiritual" believers; it was assigned to those that **believe**
- The ministry of deliverance is just as critical and relevant as the ministry of "tongues"

_____

_____

_____

_____

Matthew 21:12-15

12 And Jesus went into the temple of God, and cast out all them that sold and bought in the temple, and overthrew the tables of the moneychangers, and the seats of them that sold doves,

13 And said unto them, It is written, My house shall be called the house of prayer; but ye have made it a den of thieves.

14 And the blind and the lame came to him in the temple; and he healed them.

15 And when the chief priests and scribes saw the wonderful things that he did, and the children crying in the temple, and saying, Hosanna to the Son of David; they were sore displeased,

- The setting in this passage is not out in the world, it is "in" the temple. - The temple had different "areas": Outer Court, Inner Court (Holy Place), and the Holy of Holies
- If there is a problem in one of the areas, the whole temple had a problem. They were not exchanging money in the Holy of Holies.
- Once the temple had been cleansed (deliverance), healing and other miracles flowed
-

Consider 1 Corinthians 3:16

_____

_____

_____

***In order for an effective and accurate deliverance session to occur, there should be an element of the "prophetic" involved.

- Word of Knowledge

- Word of Wisdom

- Spirit of Discernment

WORD STUDY

SPIRIT (n)

1. An animating or vital principle held to give life to physical organisms
2. A malevolent being that enters and possesses a human being
3. The force within a person that is believed to give the body life, energy, and power
4. The immaterial intelligent or sentient part of a person

SPIRIT (HEBREW)

1. **H7307 - RÛACH** = wind; breath; mind; air
2. **H5397 - NESHÂMÂH** = breath; spirit; a puff; a blast

SPIRIT (GREEK)

1. **G4151 - PNEUMA** = a current of air; wind; spirit;
2. **G4152 - PNEUMATIKOS =** non-carnal; spiritual
3. **G1140 - DAIMONION** = an evil spirit; a demon

DELIVER (v)

1. To set free
2. To assist in the birth of; to give birth to
3. To disburden (oneself of thoughts, opinions, etc…)
4. To hand over, transfer, or surrender
5. To release or rescue (from captivity, harm, corruption, etc…)

DELIVERANCE (n)

1. The act or instance of delivering

DELIVER (HEBREW)

1. **H5337 - *NATSAL* =** to strip; plunder; deliver oneself; be delivered; snatch away; deliver
2. **H346 - *YASHA* =** to deliver; to save
3. **H6403 - *PALAT* =** to escape; to deliver; bring into security; to slip out
4. **H6561 - *PARAQ* =** to tear apart or away; separate, split

DELIVER (GREEK)

1. **G4506 - *RHUOMAI* =** draw to oneself; deliver
2. **G1807 - *EXAIREÓ* =** to take out, to deliver
3. **G525 - *APALLASSÓ* =** to remove; release; be "legally transferred out"
4. **G4982 - *SÓZÓ* =** to save; heal, preserve, rescue
5. **G1659 - *ELEUTHEROÓ* =** to make free; set free; liberate

CAST OUT (HEBREW/GREEK)

1. **H1644 - *GARASH* =** to drive out; cast out; expel; to drive out from a possession
2. **H3423 - *YARASH* OR *YARESH* =** to take possession of, inherit, dispossess; seize
3. **G1544 - *EKBALLO* =** I throw; cast out; put out; banish; expel; bring forth, produce; tear out; cause a thing to move straight on to its intended goal; eject

POSSESSED

G1139 - *DAIMONIZOMAI* = to be possessed by a demon; under the power of a demon (fallen angel); to be exercised by a demon

1. Spurred or moved by a strong feeling, madness, or a supernatural power

2. To have as belonging to one; have as property; own

3. To maintain control over

4. Under the influence of a powerful force, such as a spirit or strong emotion

KEYS TO REMEMBER

*** Deliverance is an action and function of The Kingdom

*** Deliverance must be approached and accomplished via love –

*** DEMONS HATE LOVE!!!

*** Deliverance ministry mandates and necessitates humility and team work

*** Prophets are to work in conjunction with other giftings /offices – not independently

*** Position before Power

_____

_____

_____

_____

_____

_____

_____

_____

*** The soul is the object of the war.

*** The mind is often the first target and the primary battlefield.

*** Lies based on words heard and our experiences start to shape and dominate our thought life.

Stronghold = when a demonic spirit has the ability to consistently speak a lie and provoke a negative or sinful response in us. It is a fortified and resistant thought or lie.

*** A lie is at the root of every stronghold and bondage!!!

_____

_____

_____

_____

_____

_____

_____

When demons form strongholds in our lives, they target the soul. However, before they can build strongholds they need an access point —a way into the soul. Most access points can be divided into four general categories. This is not inclusive, nor the only paths to enter, these are the most commonly observed:

1. Trauma   2. The five senses   3. Deception   4. Generational sins

*** The most important thing to notice is that all four categories involve sin, whether voluntary or involuntary. We must remember that we live in a "fallen world". Sin is the only thing that gives an unclean spirit the right to enter and remain in our lives.

_____

_____

_____

_____

_____

_____

Trauma (n):

1.   An injury (such as a wound) to living tissue caused by an extrinsic agent

2.   A disordered psychic or behavioral state resulting from severe mental or emotional stress or physical injury

3.   A very difficult or unpleasant experience that causes someone to have mental or emotional problems usually for a long time

Greek "*traumat*"- trauma wound; alteration of trōma; akin to Greek *titrōskein* to wound, *tetrainein* to pierce

_____

_____

_____

_____

_____

_____

The 5 Senses (Traditionally Recognized)

1. Sight (ophthalmoception)

2. Hearing (audioception)

3. Taste (gustaoception)

4. Smell (olfacoception or olfacception)

5. Touch (tactioception)

...are the five traditionally recognized.

_____

_____

_____

_____

_____

_____

Deception (n):

1. the act of causing someone to accept as true or valid what is false or invalid

2. the act of making someone believe something that is not true

3. something that deceives or is intended to deceive; fraud; artifice

Deceive (v):

1. To mislead by a false appearance or statement; delude; deliberate misrepresentation

2. To mislead or falsely persuade others

3. To cause to accept as true or valid what is false or invalid

HEBREW /GREEK

H6601 - "PÂTHÂH" - "paw-thaw' = to *open*, that is, *be* (causatively *make*) *roomy*; usually figuratively (in a mental or moral sense) to *be* (causatively *make*) *simple* or (in a sinister way) *delude:* - allure, deceive, enlarge, entice, flatter, persuade, silly (one).
H5377 - "NÂSHÂ'" - naw-shaw'; to *lead astray*, that is, (mentally) to *delude*, or (morally) to *seduce*
G4105 - "PLANAŌ" - to (properly *cause* to) roam (from safety, truth, or virtue): - go astray, deceive, err, seduce, wander, be out of the way.

_____

_____

_____

_____

Generational Sins/Curses - Ex 34:7; Lam 5:7; Jer 31:29-30; Gal 3:13

1. A defilement that was passed down from one generation to another.
2. Living under bondage that the sins of their forefathers.

Examples:

1. A continual negative pattern of something being handed down from generation to generation
2. Family illnesses that seem to just walk from one person down to the next (cancer is a common physical manifestation of a spiritual bondage)
3. Continual financial difficulties (they continually hit roadblocks in their finances)
4. Mental problems, persistent irrational fears and depression

It is possible for demons to enter a child before he accepts Jesus, then remain dormant or hidden in that child's life until some time later in his or her life when it manifests (or makes itself known)

The curse may be canceled, but the demons may remain

_____

_____

_____

FINAL POINTS TO CONSIDER

Demons vs Discipline

Identity and Authority

Timing

Individual vs Corporate

_____

_____

_____

_____

_____

_____

THE DELIVERANCE PROCESS

1. Communicate

2. Cancel

3. Command

4. Cleanse

5. Counsel

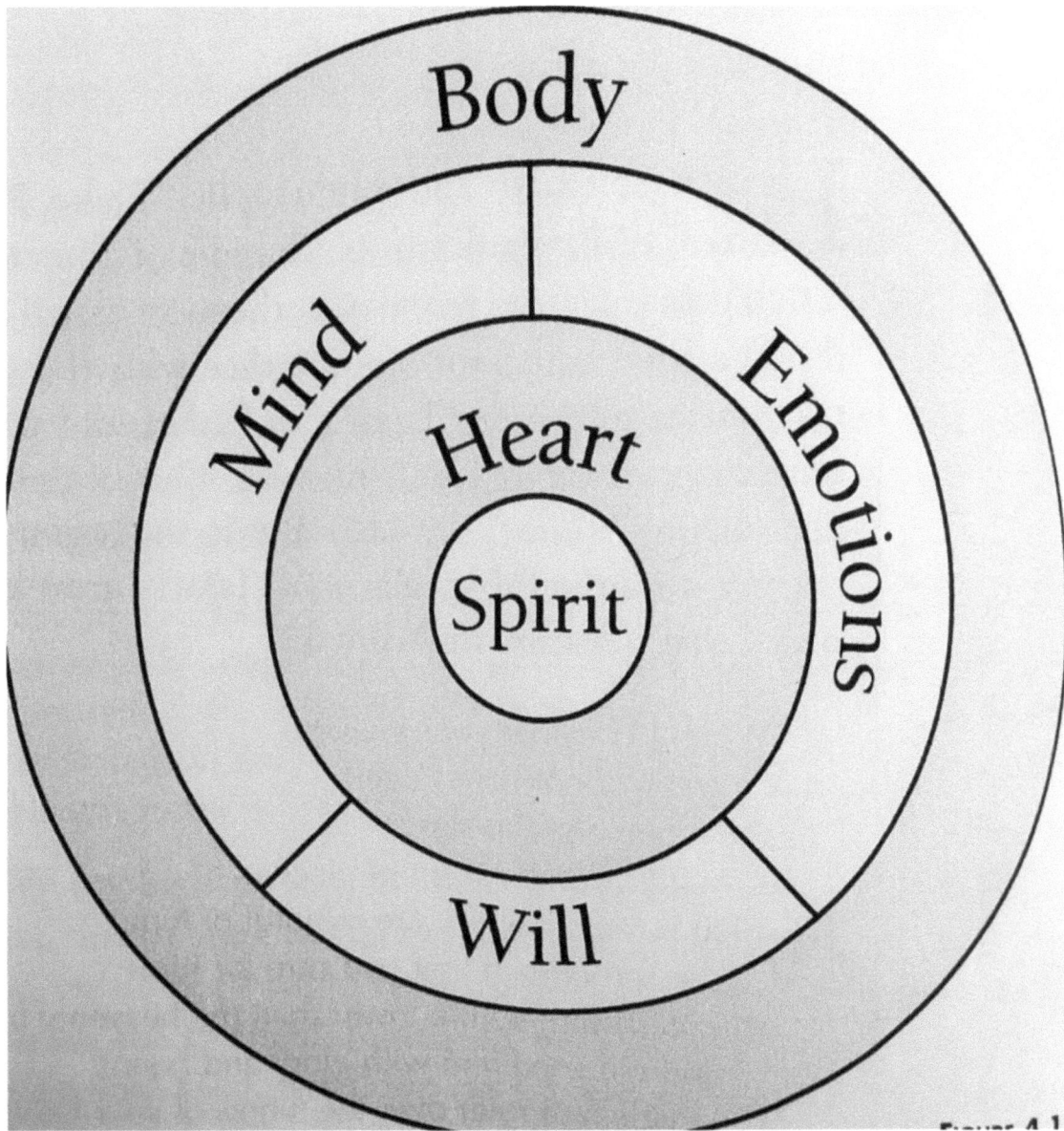

Figure 4.1

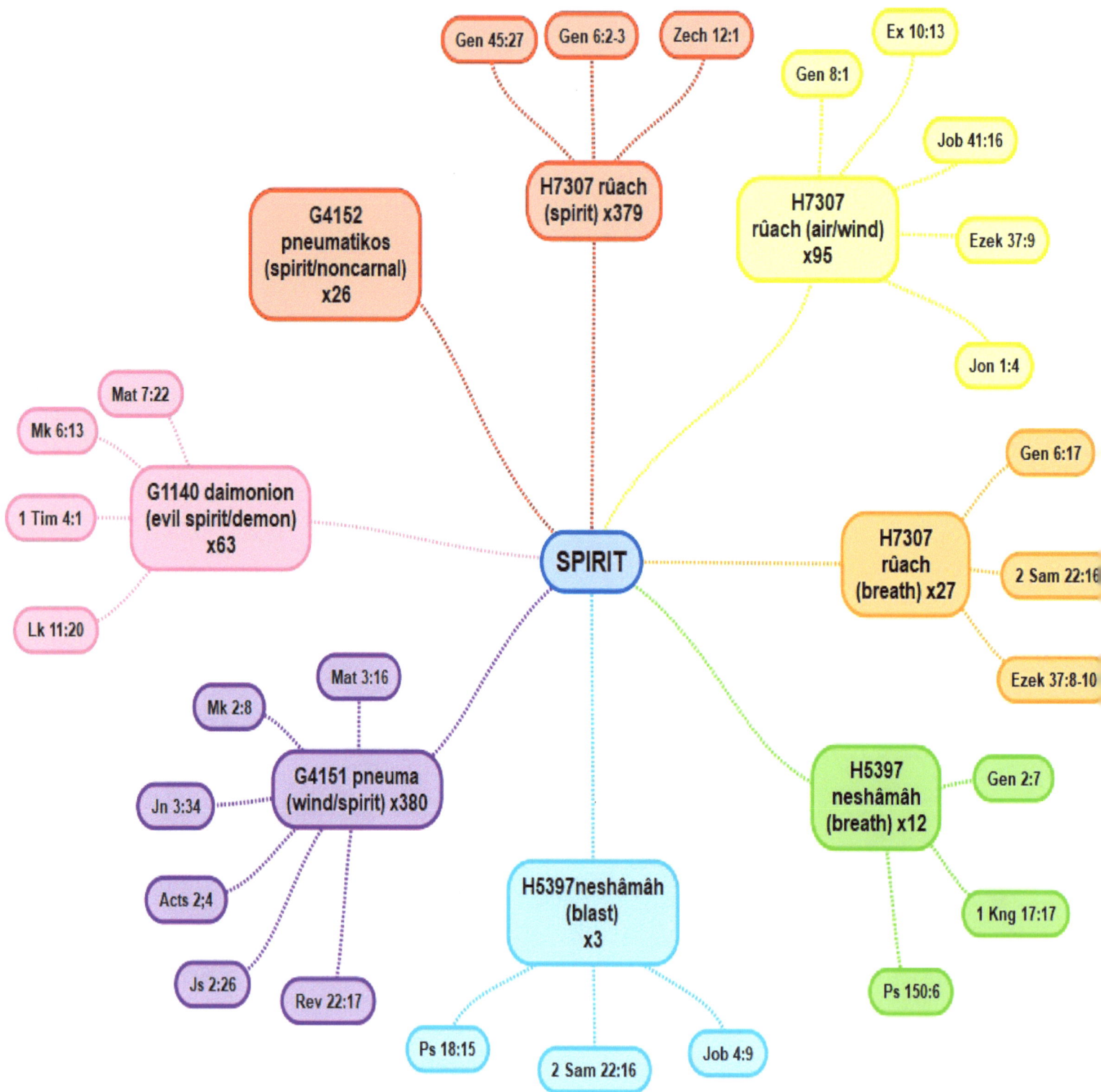

SPIRIT

H7307 rûach (spirit) x379
- Gen 45:27
- Gen 6:2-3
- Zech 12:1

H7307 rûach (air/wind) x95
- Gen 8:1
- Ex 10:13
- Job 41:16
- Ezek 37:9
- Jon 1:4

G4152 pneumatikos (spirit/noncarnal) x26

G1140 daimonion (evil spirit/demon) x63
- Mat 7:22
- Mk 6:13
- 1 Tim 4:1
- Lk 11:20

H7307 rûach (breath) x27
- Gen 6:17
- 2 Sam 22:16
- Ezek 37:8-10

G4151 pneuma (wind/spirit) x380
- Mat 3:16
- Mk 2:8
- Jn 3:34
- Acts 2;4
- Js 2:26
- Rev 22:17

H5397 neshâmâh (blast) x3
- Ps 18:15
- 2 Sam 22:16
- Job 4:9

H5397 neshâmâh (breath) x12
- Gen 2:7
- 1 Kng 17:17
- Ps 150:6

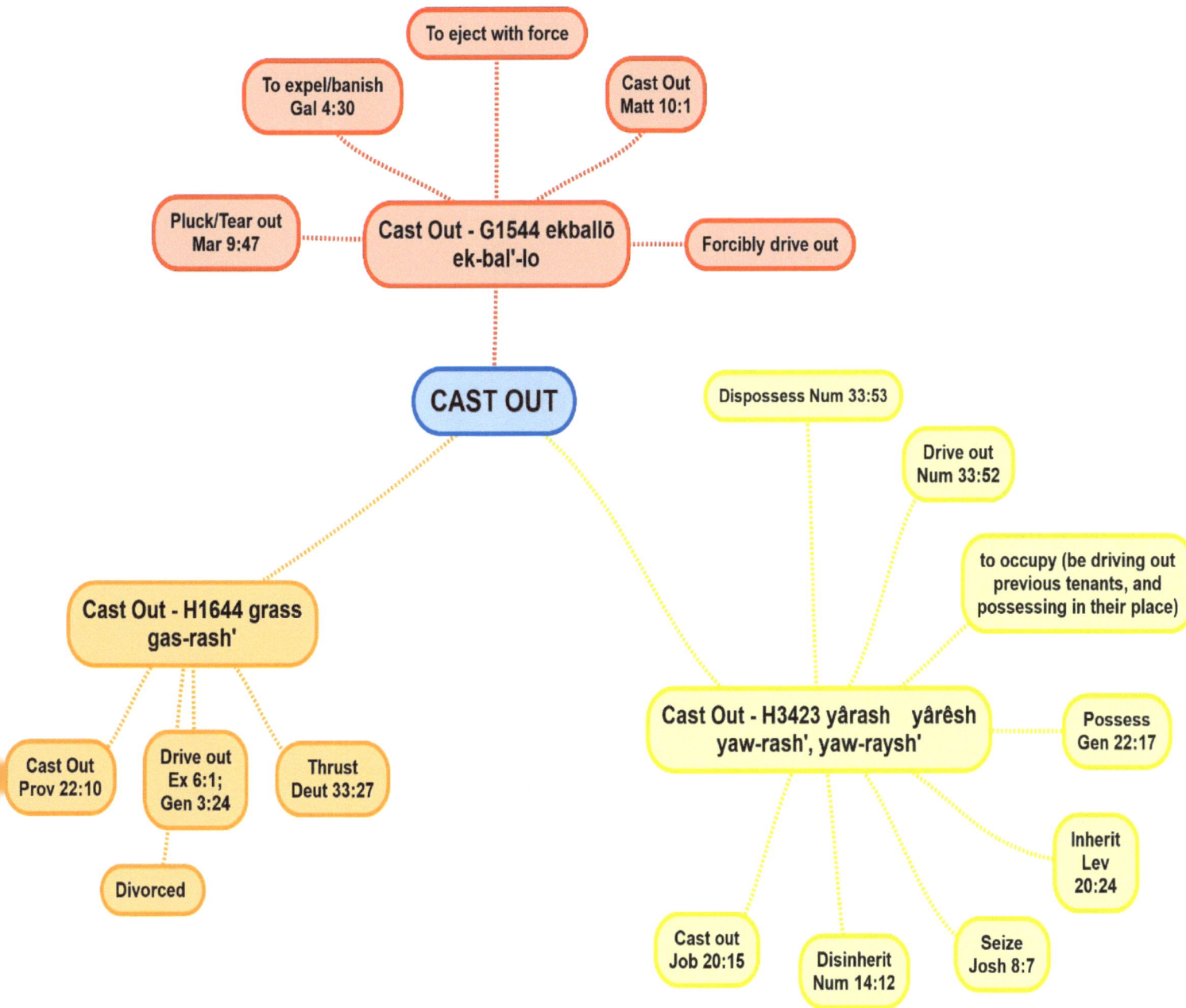

CAST OUT

Cast Out - G1544 ekballō ek-bal'-lo

- To eject with force
- To expel/banish Gal 4:30
- Cast Out Matt 10:1
- Pluck/Tear out Mar 9:47
- Forcibly drive out

Cast Out - H1644 grass gas-rash'

- Cast Out Prov 22:10
- Drive out Ex 6:1; Gen 3:24
  - Divorced
- Thrust Deut 33:27

Cast Out - H3423 yârash yârêsh yaw-rash', yaw-raysh'

- Dispossess Num 33:53
- Drive out Num 33:52
- to occupy (be driving out previous tenants, and possessing in their place)
- Possess Gen 22:17
- Inherit Lev 20:24
- Seize Josh 8:7
- Disinherit Num 14:12
- Cast out Job 20:15

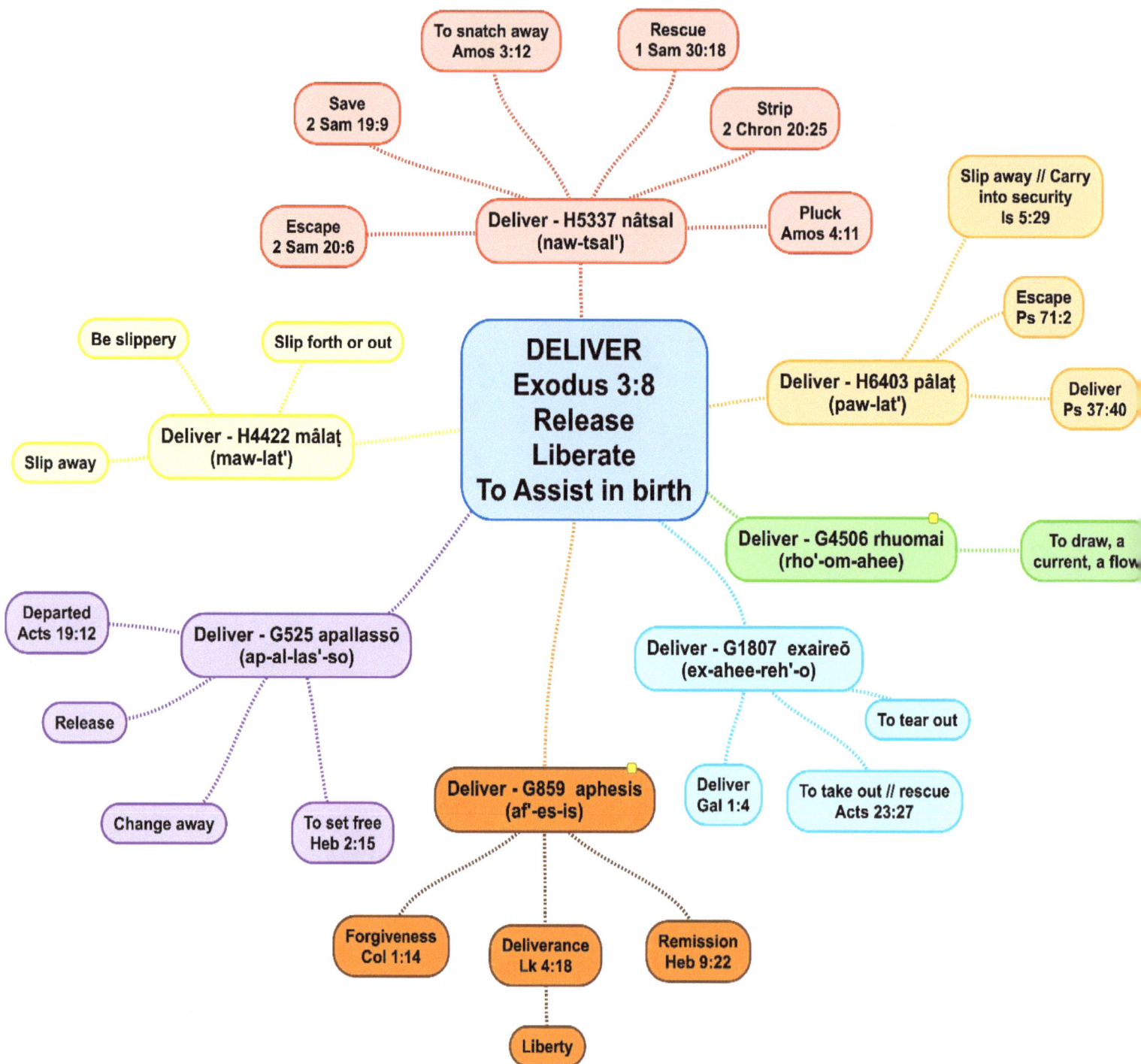

DELIVER
Exodus 3:8
Release
Liberate
To Assist in birth

Deliver - H5337 nâtsal (naw-tsal')
- To snatch away — Amos 3:12
- Rescue — 1 Sam 30:18
- Save — 2 Sam 19:9
- Strip — 2 Chron 20:25
- Escape — 2 Sam 20:6
- Pluck — Amos 4:11

Deliver - H6403 pâlaṭ (paw-lat')
- Slip away // Carry into security — Is 5:29
- Escape — Ps 71:2
- Deliver — Ps 37:40

Deliver - H4422 mâlaṭ (maw-lat')
- Be slippery
- Slip forth or out
- Slip away

Deliver - G4506 rhuomai (rho'-om-ahee)
- To draw, a current, a flow

Deliver - G525 apallassō (ap-al-las'-so)
- Departed — Acts 19:12
- Release
- Change away
- To set free — Heb 2:15

Deliver - G1807 exaireō (ex-ahee-reh'-o)
- To tear out
- Deliver — Gal 1:4
- To take out // rescue — Acts 23:27

Deliver - G859 aphesis (af'-es-is)
- Forgiveness — Col 1:14
- Deliverance — Lk 4:18
- Liberty
- Remission — Heb 9:22

Incipient – Prophetic Course Level 1

CHRISTIAN T. HOWELL SR.

PROPHETIC CULTURE

Culture - the customary beliefs, social forms, and material traits of a racial, religious, or social group

-        the set of shared attitudes, values, goals, and practices that characterizes an institution or organization

-        a way of thinking, behaving, or working that exists in a place or organization (such as a business)

1 SAMUEL 10:5-11

5 After that thou shalt come to the hill of God, where is the garrison of the Philistines: and it shall come to pass, when thou art come thither to the city, that thou shalt meet a company of prophets coming down from the high place with a psaltery, and a tabret, and a pipe, and a harp, before them; and they shall prophesy:

6 And the Spirit of the LORD will come upon thee, and thou shalt prophesy with them, and shalt be turned into another man.

7 And let it be, when these signs are come unto thee, that thou do as occasion serve thee; for God is with thee.

8 And thou shalt go down before me to Gilgal; and, behold, I will come down unto thee, to offer burnt offerings, and to sacrifice sacrifices of peace offerings: seven days shalt thou tarry, till I come to thee, and shew thee what thou shalt do.

9 And it was so, that when he had turned his back to go from Samuel, God gave him another heart: and all those signs came to pass that day.

10 And when they came thither to the hill, behold, a company of prophets met him; and the Spirit of God came upon him, and he prophesied among them.

11 And it came to pass, when all that knew him beforetime saw that, behold, he prophesied among the prophets, then the people said one to another, What is this that is come unto the son of Kish? Is Saul also among the prophets?

_____

_____

_____

_____

_____

1 SAMUEL 19:18-24

18 So David fled, and escaped, and came to Samuel to Ramah, and told him all that Saul had done to him. And he and Samuel went and dwelt in Naioth.

19 And it was told Saul, saying, Behold, David is at Naioth in Ramah.

20 And Saul sent messengers to take David: and when they saw the company of the prophets prophesying, and Samuel standing as appointed over them, the Spirit of God was upon the messengers of Saul, and they also prophesied.

21 And when it was told Saul, he sent other messengers, and they prophesied likewise. And Saul sent messengers again the third time, and they prophesied also.

22 Then went he also to Ramah, and came to a great well that is in Sechu: and he asked and said, Where are Samuel and David? And one said, Behold, they be at Naioth in Ramah.

23 And he went thither to Naioth in Ramah: and the Spirit of God was upon him also, and he went on, and prophesied, until he came to Naioth in Ramah.

24 And he stripped off his clothes also, and prophesied before Samuel in like manner, and lay down naked all that day and all that night. Wherefore they say, Is Saul also among the prophets?

_____

_____

_____

_____

_____

_____

1 CORINTHIANS 14:1

(**KJV**) Follow after charity, and desire spiritual gifts, but rather that ye may prophesy.

(**AMP**) Pursue [this] love [with eagerness, make it your goal], yet earnestly desire and cultivate the spiritual gifts [to be used by believers for the benefit of the church], but especially that you may [a]prophesy [to foretell the future, to speak a new message from God to the people].

(**GW**) Pursue love, and desire spiritual gifts, but especially the gift of speaking what God has revealed.

_____

_____

_____

_____

_____

_____

_____

Numbers 11:29 And Moses said unto him, Enviest thou for my sake? would God that all the LORD'S people were prophets, and that the LORD would put his spirit upon them!

_____

_____

_____

_____

_____

Amos 3:8 The lion hath roared, who will not fear? the Lord GOD hath spoken, who can but prophesy?

_____

_____

_____

_____

_____

KEYS TO REMEMBER

Prophets (prophetic people) are builders and always build in the local church…

Prophets (prophetic people) are worshippers

Prophets are intercessors but not all intercessors are prophets

Prophets (prophetic people) are to work in conjunction with other giftings/offices – not independently

Judge the prophecy more than the person delivering

Prophecy can create or confirm

PROPHET (HEBREW)

NABI = to bubble forth (like a fountain)

ROEH = seer, prophet, vision, oracle

CHOZEH = seer

MASSA = what is lifted up, a burden, message or song

NATAPH = to cause to drop, let drop; to pour out like honey from the mouth of a lover; the word that drops down like rain

SHAMMAR = keep, keep watch or preserve; to cultivate and guard

QOWL = aloud, bleating, cry out, lightness, lowing, noise, peaceful small voice, proclaim, to sing a song, a spark, thundering

CHAZOWN = a fountain or well with living, moving water

CHAZOWTH = revelation

PROPHET (GREEK)

PROPHETES = one who speaks for another, especially one who speaks for a God and so interprets His will to man an interpreter; to foretell & forthtell

THEOPNEUSTOS = God-breathed – referring to the divine inspiration (in-breathing

APOKALUPIS = revelation, appearing, coming, manifest, be revealed

THE WORD OF THE LORD (HEBREW)

THE PEH OF YAWEH = the blowing, mind, mouth, words, speech; the Word of God that come directly out of the mouth of God (now)

THE IMRAH OF YAWEH = the saying, speech, word, or commandment; the Word that comes from Him speaking His commands & decrees

THE DABAR OF YAWEH = a glorious word, to speak with power, an authoritative word, a word which is logical and reasonable; a cause

WORD – "DABAR" (HEBREW) = Word of the Lord that can confront and challenge kings, rulers, and leaders of the earth

SELAH (HEWBREW) = to be silent or still; to cease from speaking; a pause in order to think of what God has spoken or done for you

SHAMEA (HEBREW) = to hear and obey; to listen to words and rebukes of the wise; to summon

THREE ADMINISTRATIONS OF THE PROPHETIC

1. The spirit of prophecy

Acts 2:17-18; Joel 2:28-29; 1 Samuel 10:10-11

_____

_____

_____

2. The gift of prophecy

1 Cor 12:1-11; Romans 12:4-8; 1 Cor 14:1; 2 Tim 1:6

_____

_____

_____

3. The office of a prophet

Deut 18:18; Eph 4:11-13; 1 Cor 12:28

_____

_____

_____

BASIC PURPOSE OF PROPHECY

1 Corinthians 14:3

(**KJV**) But he that prophesieth speaketh unto men to **edification**, and **exhortation**, and **comfort**.

(**AMP**) But [on the other hand] the one who prophesies speaks to people for **edification [to promote their spiritual growth]** and [speaks words of] **encouragement [to uphold and advise them concerning the matters of God]** and [speaks words of] **consolation [to compassionate comfort them]**.

_____

_____

_____

_____

Scriptures to Explore

Joel 2:28 - And it shall come to pass afterward, that I will pour out my spirit upon all flesh; and your sons and your daughters shall prophesy, your old men shall dream dreams, your young men shall see visions:

_____

_____

_____

Acts 2:3 - And there appeared unto them cloven tongues like as of fire, and it sat upon each of them.

_____

_____

_____

1 Corinthians 14:1, 39

1 Follow after charity, and desire spiritual gifts, but rather that ye may prophesy.

39 Wherefore, brethren, covet to prophesy, and forbid not to speak with tongues.

_____

_____

_____

Numbers 11:25-29

25 And the Lord came down in a cloud, and spake unto him, and took of the spirit that was upon him, and gave it unto the seventy elders: and it came to pass, that, when the spirit rested upon them, they prophesied, and did not cease.

26 But there remained two of the men in the camp, the name of the one was Eldad, and the name of the other Medad: and the spirit rested upon them; and they were of them that were written, but went not out unto the tabernacle: and they prophesied in the camp.

27 And there ran a young man, and told Moses, and said, Eldad and Medad do prophesy in the camp.

28 And Joshua the son of Nun, the servant of Moses, one of his young men, answered and said, My lord Moses, forbid them.

29 And Moses said unto him, Enviest thou for my sake? would God that all the Lord's people were prophets, and that the Lord would put his spirit upon them!

_____

_____

_____

_____

_____

_____

1 Corinthians 14:29-33

29 Let the prophets speak two or three, and let the other judge.

30 If any thing be revealed to another that sitteth by, let the first hold his peace.

31 For ye may all prophesy one by one, that all may learn, and all may be comforted.

32 And the spirits of the prophets are subject to the prophets.

33 For God is not the author of confusion, but of peace, as in all churches of the saints.

_____

_____

_____

_____

_____

_____

_____

BARRIERS IN THE CULTURE

1 CORINTHIANS 12:1

(KJV) Now concerning spiritual gifts, brethren, I would not have you ignorant.

(AMP) Now about the spiritual gifts [the special endowments given by the Holy Spirit], brothers and sisters, I do not want you to be uninformed.

_____

_____

_____

1 CORINTHIANS 13:1-2

1 Though I speak with the tongues of men and of angels, and have not charity, I am become as sounding brass, or a tinkling cymbal.

2 And though I have the gift of prophecy, and understand all mysteries, and all knowledge; and though I have all faith, so that I could remove mountains, and have not charity, I am nothing.

_____

_____

_____

GALATIANS 5:6

For in Jesus Christ neither circumcision availeth any thing, nor uncircumcision; but faith which worketh by love.

ROMANS 12:6

Having then gifts differing according to the grace that is given to us, whether prophecy, let us prophesy according to the proportion of faith;

ROMANS 10:17

So then faith cometh by hearing, and hearing by the word of God.

AMOS 3:8

The lion hath roared, who will not fear? the Lord God hath spoken, who can but prophesy?

_____

_____

_____

PSALMS 46:10-11

10 He says, "Be still, and know that I am God; I will be exalted among the nations, I will be exalted in the earth."

11 The Lord Almighty is with us; the God of Jacob is our fortress.

PSALMS 37:7

Rest in the Lord, and wait patiently for him: fret not thyself because of him who prospereth in his way, because of the man who bringeth wicked devices to pass.

_____

_____

_____

Here are different ways that God may communicate with you:

1. Impressions

2. Dreams

3. Visions

4. Still Small Voice

5. Preached Messages

6. Signs and Wonders

7. World Events/Situations

Prophetic Protocol

1. Always prophesy in love (1 Cor 14:1).

2. Prophesy according to the proportion of your faith (Rom 12:6)

3. Avoid being too flashy, demonstrative, theatrical, or dramatic

4. Opposite sex – inappropriate touch and language

5. Stay humble…people should only worship Him.

6. Don't be a lone-ranger or a prophetic hog.

7. Eliminate excessive hand motions; and movements such as rocking back and forth. ALSO, do not speak in tongues excessively while prophesying.

8. Never release a prophetic word that goes contrary to His Word (scripture).

9. Know your strengths and limitations.***Your measure of grace***

10. The spirit of the prophet is subject to the prophet (1 Cor 14:32). God will never give you something that you cannot control.

11. Do not be repetitious while prophesying. Stop when the Holy Spirit stops.

12. Use recording devices when possible. It provides accountability and gives the ability to be judged.

13. Speak in the first person. You are representing the Voice of the Lord on the earth.

What Prophets & Prophetic People Love

1. The presence of God (Ps 63:2)

2. The bruised and the hurt (Is 42:3-4)

3. Worship - Israel's worship was established by prophets (1Chron 25:1-6 & 2 Chron 29:25)

4. Liberty/Freedom (2 Cor 3:17)

5. Rhema (Mat 4:4) - ***Inspired teaching/preaching

What Prophets Hate

1. Injustice & Hypocrisy (Mat 23:14)

2. Crookedness/Perversion (Ecc 1:15)

3. Mixture/Compromise (Is 1:22 & Hos 7:8)

4. Traditions of men (Mat 15:3 & Mk 7:13)

5. Control & Witchcraft (Mic 5:12)

6. False Prophets (Gifts) (Mat 7:15-16)

7. Ignorance (Hos 4:6 & Is 5:13)

Final Words

The prophetic is God's way of giving hope, reminding His children that they have a future, and the way towards it.

Prophets & Prophetic Community are a sign of presence and blessings (Ps 74:9, 1 Sam 3:1, & Amos 8:11-12)

> *****The prophetic breaks famine*****

Prophets & Prophetic Community reveal God's plan (Amos 3:7 & Eph 3:5,9)

Prophets are taught by God (Jn 7:15)

The majority of a prophet's ministry is led in secret (Mat 6:6 & Mk 1:35)

A prophet (or prophetic person) is a vessel…

> **Vessels need purging** (Prov 25:4 & Is 6:5)
> **Vessels are chosen by God** (1 Cor 1:27-29 & 15:10)

Healthy and effective prophetic administration is a major aspect to seeing heaven released on earth!!!

PROPHET

Watchman - Shamar (H8104)
- Protector
- Guard
- Bodyguard
- Doorkeeper

Prophet - Nabi (H5030)
- Inspired Man
- Spokesman
- Prophet
- One Who Announces or Pours Forth the Declarations of God.

Seer - Chozeh (H2374)
- Beholder in a Vision
- Seer
- Prophet
- Adviser
- Counselor
- One Who Has Insight

Prophet - Nataph (H5197)
- Ooze
- Fall in Drops
- Speak by Inspiration
- To Preach

Prophet - Prophetes (G4396)
- One Who Speaks for a God
- Foreteller
- Inspired Speaker
- Interpreter

Seer - Roeh (H7203)
- Prophet
- A Revealer of Secrets
- Prophetic Vision

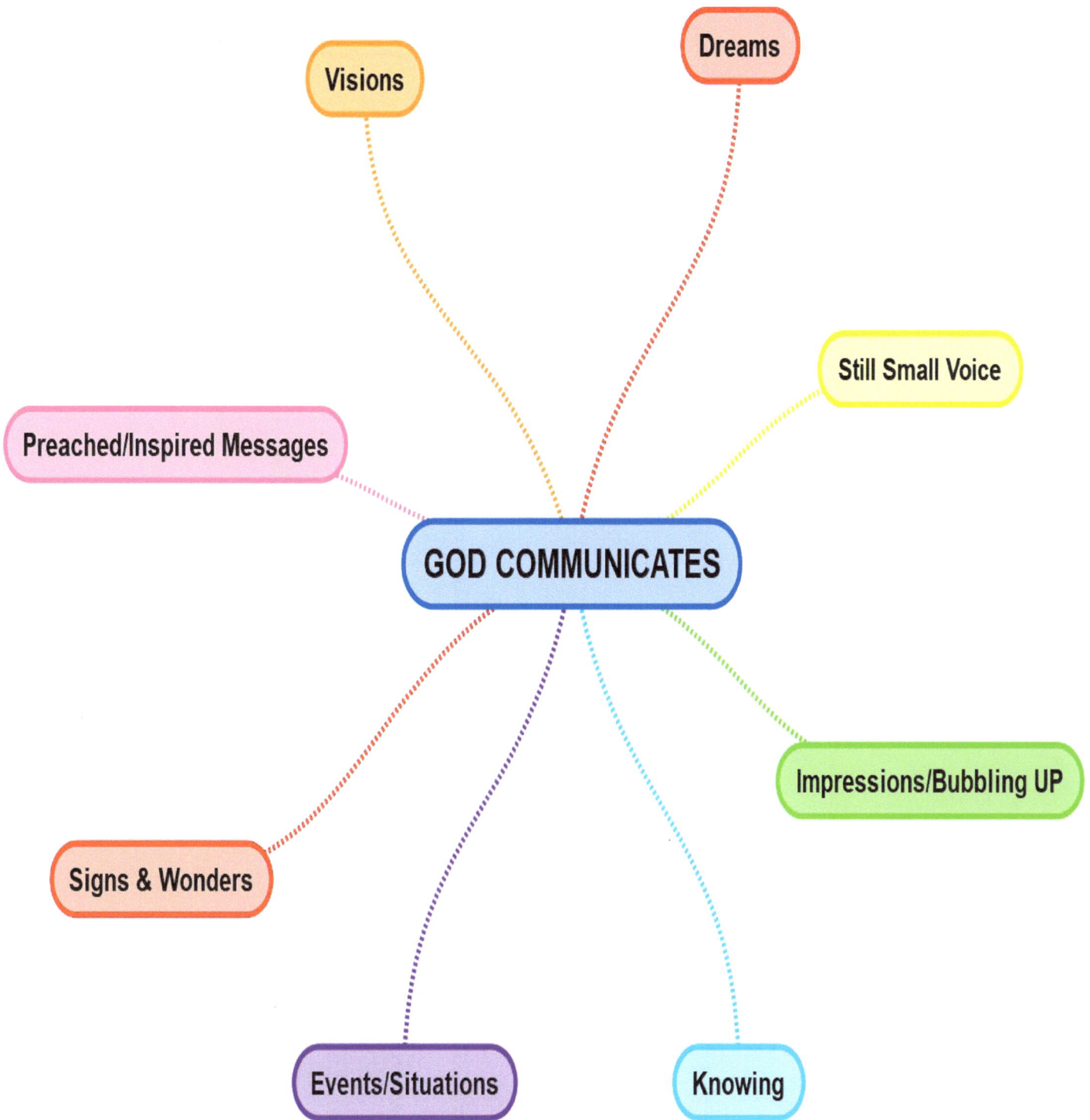

Visions

Dreams

Still Small Voice

Preached/Inspired Messages

GOD COMMUNICATES

Impressions/Bubbling UP

Signs & Wonders

Events/Situations

Knowing

HOW PROPHETS FUNCTION/DESCRIPTION

- Know When Things Are Off
- Concerned about God's Agenda
- Love Purity
- Hate Mixture
- Great at Releasing
- Weep
- Make Impartations
- Great Intercessors
- Cannot be Bought
- Identify Evil People/Motives
- Friends of God
- Great Psalmist & Minstrels
- Love Glory
- Sensitive to the Spirit Realm

www.ingramcontent.com/pod-product-compliance
Lightning Source LLC
Chambersburg PA
CBHW060900270326
41935CB00004B/52